STRANGE
BUT
TRUE

Weird stories from the wacky world of sports

CONTENTS

Crazy Games, p. 4

4 Crazy Games

8 Olympic Tales

10 Pranks and Tricks

14 The Winning Edge

19 Fan-tastic Antics

Pranks and Tricks, p. 10

Animals and Mascots, p. 22

Bad Luck, p. 26

Nicknames, p. 31

22 Animals and Mascots

24 Weird Weather

26 Bad Luck

29 Major Mishaps

31 Nicknames

CRAZY GAMES

Some sports are full of wild and crazy finishes. Others are just plain wild.

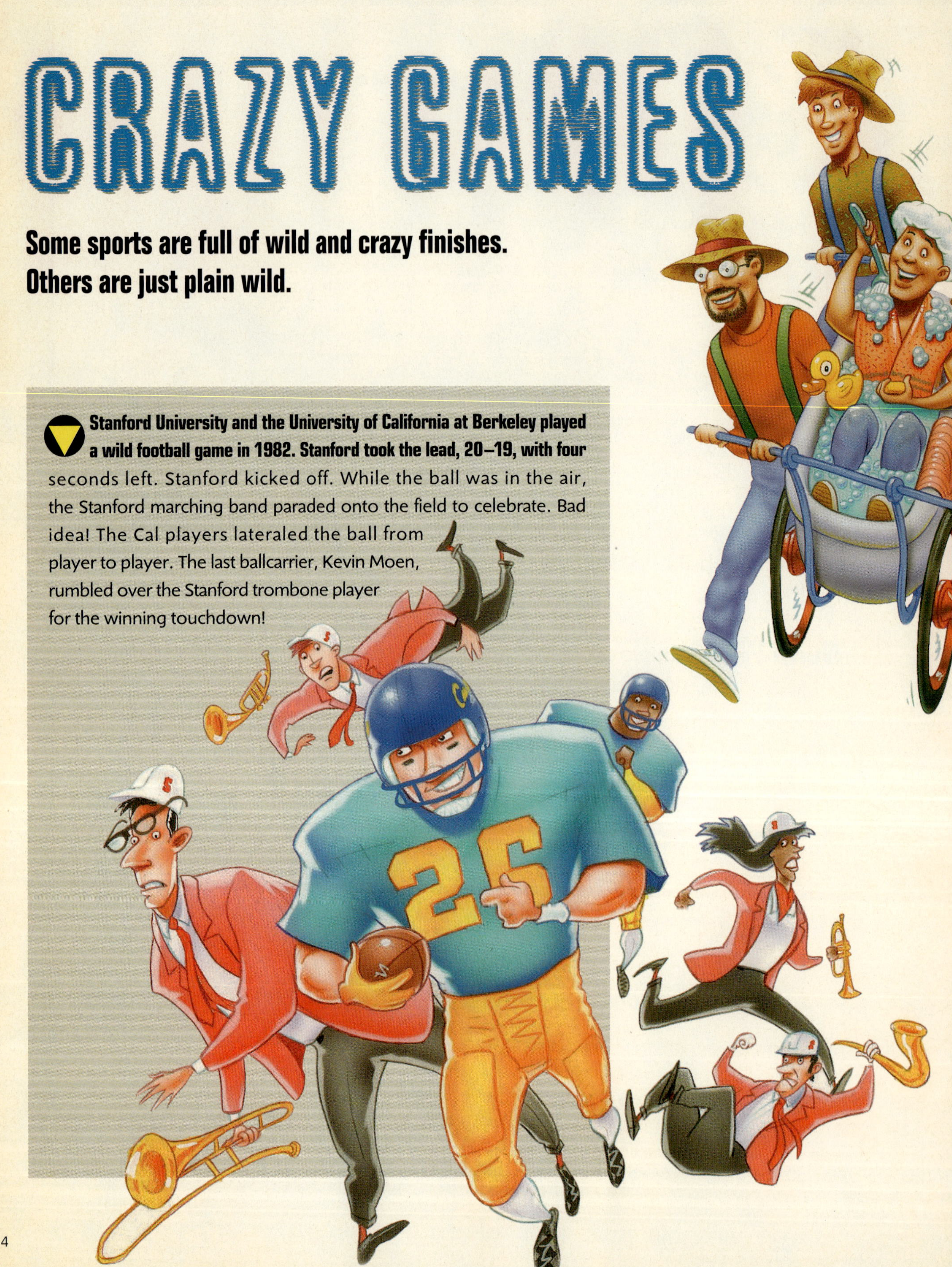

Stanford University and the University of California at Berkeley played a wild football game in 1982. Stanford took the lead, 20–19, with four seconds left. Stanford kicked off. While the ball was in the air, the Stanford marching band paraded onto the field to celebrate. Bad idea! The Cal players lateraled the ball from player to player. The last ballcarrier, Kevin Moen, rumbled over the Stanford trombone player for the winning touchdown!

◀ **Rub-a-dub-dub, look out for the speeding tub.** Welcome to the Great Bathtub Race of Nome, Alaska. Four people push a "racetub" on wheels for about five city blocks. Each tub is filled with a passenger, a bar of soap, a towel, a bath mat, and at least 10 gallons of soapy water. Five tubs race at once. The first team to cross the finish line wins!

▼ **"There's no arm in toe wrestling!" That's the** slogan of the toe-wrestling world championships. The contest is held each year in Wetton, England. Two wrestlers sit and place one foot on the "toes rack." They lock toes and each tries to pin his opponent's foot to the mat. Alan "Nasty" Nash is *toe*-rific! He is a four-time world champ.

▲ **The New York Knicks were leading the Indiana** Pacers, 105–99, with 18.7 seconds left in a 1995 playoff game. No one thought the Pacers could win the game — no one except Reggie Miller, the Pacers' sharpshooting guard. Reggie scored 8 points in 8.9 seconds! The Pacers won, 107–105.

The New York Giants and Chicago Cubs were tied, 1–1, in the bottom of the ninth inning of a game in 1908. The Giants had runners on first and third with two outs when Al Bridwell hit a single. The runner at third scored easily. But Fred Merkle, the runner on first, freaked out when fans ran onto the field to celebrate. Fred fled to the clubhouse. The Cubs tagged second for a force out, wiping out the winning run. The game ended in a tie when fans refused to leave the field!

Linebacker Jack Reynolds of the University of Tennessee wasn't happy after his team was ripped, 38–0, by the University of Mississippi in 1969. Jack was so steamed that he sawed an old car in half! Jack sawed for eight hours and used 14 hacksaw blades. The nickname "Hacksaw" stuck with him through college and his 15-season NFL career.

▼ **Suzy Hamilton was leading a one-mile race** in Fairfax, Virginia, in 1994. With one lap to go, she stopped running. Suzy thought the race was over and that she had won! She realized her mistake when the other runners dashed past her. But it was too late to catch up. Suzy didn't finish the race.

◀ **He shoots . . . *glub!* Competitors at the** World Underwater Hockey Championships pass and score on the bottom of a swimming pool. Six players on each side use foot-long "hockey sticks" to push the puck across the floor of the pool. The most important skill: holding your breath underwater for more than 30 seconds! Championships are held every two years.

▶ **Receiver Dayton** Carter of Marshall University was head and shoulders above West Virginia in a 1915 game. Dayton and tackle Okey Taylor ran into the end zone. Dayton hopped onto Okey's shoulders. Then Dayton caught a pass for a TD. College football outlawed the "tower play" a year later.

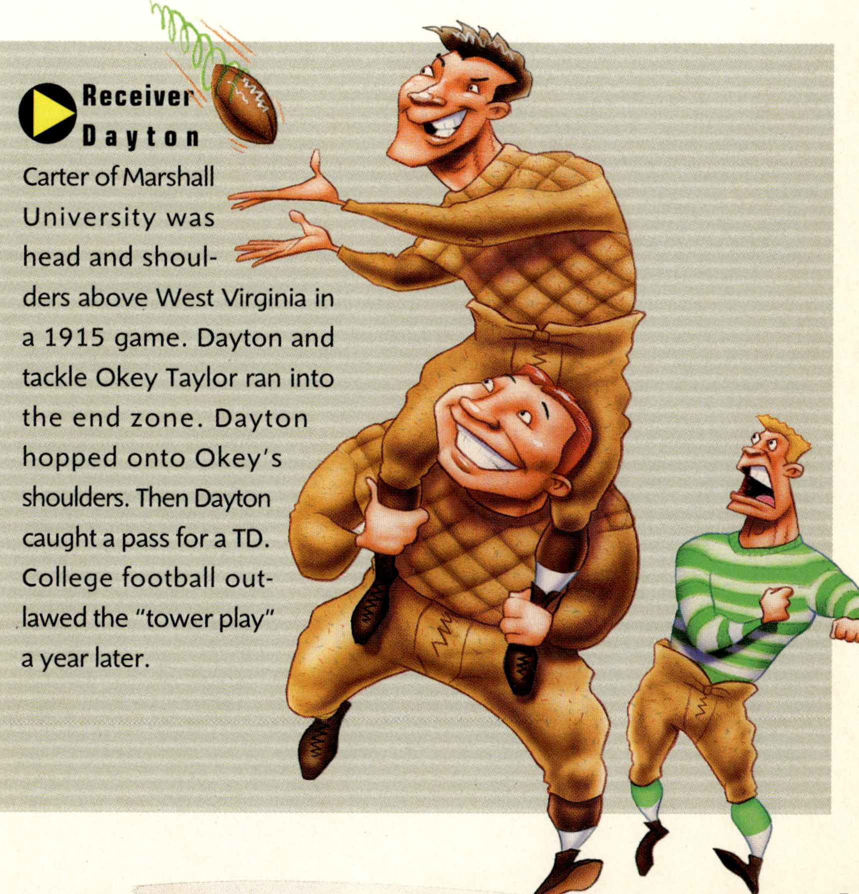

OLYMPIC TALES

The Olympics can be a real adventure — even before the Games begin!

Norway wanted to honor its national heritage when it hosted the 1994 Winter Olympics, in Lillehammer. So it lit the flame with two torches. One torch was lit with the Olympic flame in Greece. The other torch was lit by Olav Bekken, a Norwegian citizen. Olav rubbed two sticks together to start the fire that was used to light the flame. He needed six tries to get the fire going. It didn't help that a spectator conked him with a snowball!

The sun turned the speed-skating oval into slush during the 10,000-meter event at the 1948 St. Moritz (Switzerland) Games. The first skaters raced on hard, fast ice. When the track began to melt, eight skaters withdrew from the event. Buddy Solem of the U.S. skated anyway. His 26-minute 22-second time was about nine minutes behind the winner!

Cross-country ski racers need snow. But too much snow can mean trouble. Skiers in the 50-kilometer race at the 1932 Lake Placid (New York) Winter Olympics were blinded by a howling blizzard. One skier hit a rock and slid down a hill. Another broke a ski, fell, and had to be helped to his feet. A third skier crashed, hurt his shoulder, and had to be carried to the finish line. Talk about a winter *blunder*land!

The flame went on a real adventure on its way to Mexico City for the 1968 Summer Olympics. It traveled from Greece to Genoa, Italy, the birthplace of explorer Christopher Columbus. Then it went to Spain, where it was carried by one of Columbus's descendants. Next, the flame followed part of Columbus's route across the Atlantic Ocean to the New World. Finally, a relay of 17 swimmers brought the flame ashore at Veracruz, Mexico. A pair of scuba divers kept a lookout for sharks!

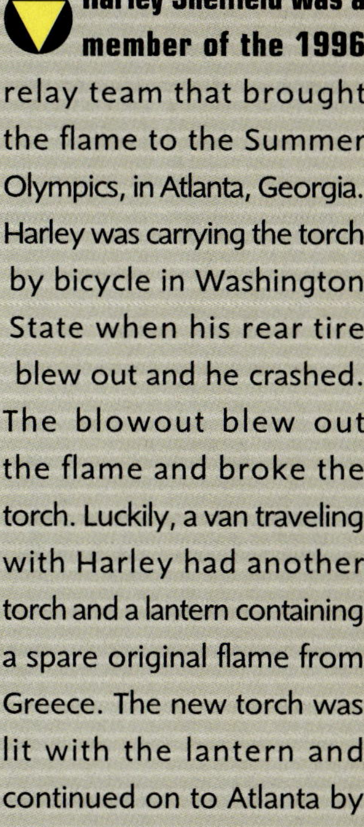

Harley Sheffield was a member of the 1996 relay team that brought the flame to the Summer Olympics, in Atlanta, Georgia. Harley was carrying the torch by bicycle in Washington State when his rear tire blew out and he crashed. The blowout blew out the flame and broke the torch. Luckily, a van traveling with Harley had another torch and a lantern containing a spare original flame from Greece. The new torch was lit with the lantern and continued on to Atlanta by motorcycle.

PRANKS AND TRICKS

Athletes are famous for playing tricks on one another. And sometimes even coaches are not above a trick or two.

▶ **Smells like team spirit!** At the 1997 Arizona Cardinals' training camp, fullback Larry Centers bagged a skunk and gave the bag to rookie quarterback Jake Plummer. Larry told Jake the bag was full of food. Jake took the bag back to his room and put it on a table. Then he went into the bathroom. When he came out, Jake found a skunk staring at him! A teammate was waiting with a video camera to tape the terrified Jake as he ran out of the room. "I was hoping not to hear sssssssss," says Jake. That would have really stunk!

▲ **Talk about making a stink! Coach Andy Landers of** the University of Georgia women's basketball team did not allow his players to wash their practice uniforms for two weeks back in 1986. Coach Landers thought the team's defense stank, and he wanted his players to know it. Oddly, the Lady Bulldogs were a sweet-smelling 15–1 at the time!

Sleeping rookies are fair game in the NHL. Winger Georges Laraque of the Edmonton Oilers made the mistake of snoozing on the team plane during his rookie season, in 1997-98. While Georges was in dreamland, his teammates went to work on him. One sprayed a can of shaving cream on his head. Another teammate snipped his tie off with scissors. When he woke up, Georges looked like a poorly dressed vanilla ice-cream cone!

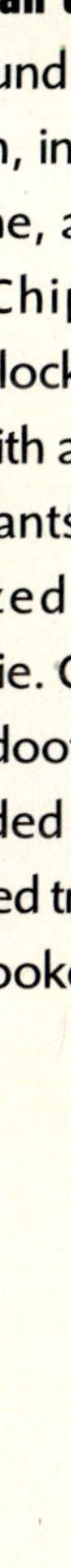

The Atlanta Braves made third baseman Chipper Jones clown around during his rookie season, in 1995. After a road game, a teammate swiped Chipper's clothes from his locker and replaced them with a clown outfit: striped pants, plaid jacket, oversized white shoes, and ugly tie. Chipper had to wear the doofy duds through a crowded airport terminal as amused travelers and teammates looked on.

Baseball players like to chew sunflower seeds and bubble gum. Rookie relief pitchers Kelly Wunsch and Kevin Beirne of the Chicago White Sox had to carry theirs in kiddie lunch boxes during the 2000 season. Veteran reliever Bill Simas ordered Kelly to carry an Elmo lunch pack. Kevin had to carry a Scooby Doo. Fans enjoyed a good laugh whenever Kelly and Kevin walked out to the bullpen before games.

U.S. hockey players Karyn Bye and Cammi Granato shared a suite with two players from Canada in graduate school. Karyn and Cammi loved to play practical jokes. Their masterpiece: covering the floor of the Canadian players' room with 600 paper cups filled with water. The players had to empty each cup before they could enter their room!

The bellhop carrying their bags into the hotel looked familiar to the San Francisco 49ers. The players had just arrived in Detroit, Michigan, for the 1982 Super Bowl. Finally, one player figured out that the bellhop was their coach, Bill Walsh! The players burst out laughing. Coach Walsh pulled the prank to help his team relax. It worked. The 49ers won the Super Bowl.

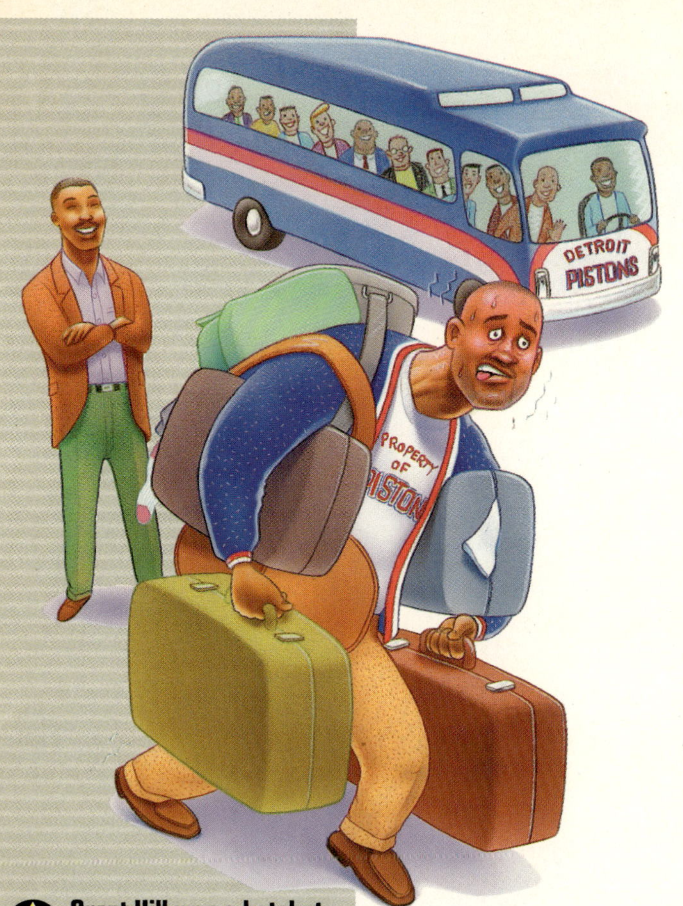

Pistons in 1994-95, but his veteran teammates weren't impressed. They made him carry their suitcases and bags into hotels on road trips. Veteran guard Joe Dumars kept an eye on Grant to make sure he kept hopping to his bellhop duties. Grant had to keep carrying bags even after he had been named an NBA All-Star. But Grant had it easier than rookie teammate Bill Curley. Bill was in charge of cleaning the locker-room showers!

▼ **The Minnesota North Stars ice hockey team** was being crushed in a game during the 1967-68 season. Coach Wren Blair was so mad after the second period that he couldn't stand to be with his players. He stormed into a closet next to the locker room. Someone accidentally closed and locked the door. Coach Blair decided to stay in the closet and let the team play the third period without him! They did — and they still lost.

THE WINNING EDGE

Athletes will sometimes do whatever it takes to get — and stay — in the game

The tough Cincinnati Bengals gave the San Diego Chargers a chill in the 1981 AFC championship game. The Chargers are from sunny California. The game was played in icy Cincinnati, Ohio. The wind-chill was 59 degrees below zero. When the Bengal offensive linemen ran onto the field wearing short-sleeved shirts, the bundled-up Chargers froze in awe. The Bengals won, 27–7.

[rah-BOS-kee] wanted batters to think he was crazy. He stomped around on the mound. He fiercely slammed the ball into his glove. He glared at batters. Sometimes he fired the ball over the batter's head on purpose. Al's wild-man act worked. He saved 76 games for the St. Louis Cardinals and Kansas City Royals between 1975 and 1979.

Sunday. With nine seconds left, Karl "The Mailman" Malone of the Utah Jazz was awarded two free throws. If he delivered, the Jazz would lead the Chicago Bulls, 84–82. As Karl got ready to shoot, Chicago's Scottie Pippen whispered, "The Mailman doesn't deliver on Sunday." Karl missed both shots!

Bailey of Canada had surgery in 1998 to repair his torn right Achilles tendon. Then he sat in a pressurized oxygen chamber. Donovan had been told he might not be able to run for a year. But the pure oxygen in the chamber helped his tendon heal fast. He was jogging eight weeks later!

Former men's tennis champ Bobby Riggs challenged women's champ Billie Jean King to a match in 1973. Bobby bragged that men were better athletes than women. But Billie Jean showed Bobby who was boss. She had four big men carry her into the Astrodome on a throne. Then she beat Bobby on the court in three sets!

Baseball gloves were invented in the 1860's. Before then, baseball players used their bare hands to catch the ball. Catchers had a particularly brutal time. Their hands were tenderized by fiery fastballs. A few catchers cooked up a solution: They slipped a slab of raw meat under a leather glove to protect their catching hand!

▼ Outfielder Jay Buhner of the Seattle Mariners made a fast, and fishy, recovery from surgery on his right elbow in 1998. After the surgery, Jay went fishing. His doctor told him to use his left arm. But Jay is a righty. Casting lefty felt clumsy, so he used his right arm. In a week, his elbow was fine.

▼ Quarterback Dan Marino of the Miami Dolphins broke his right ankle in 1996. After surgery, he wore a magnet on the ankle. Some people believe magnets increase blood flow to an injury, helping it heal. Dan missed only three games.

▲ Winger Paul Kariya of the Mighty Ducks suffered a concussion in a 1998 game. So he had needles stuck in his body to relieve the pain. This needle treatment is called acupuncture. Paul looked like a pincushion during his treatments, but his pain went away.

THE WINNING EDGE

▼ **In 1995, shortstop Dale Brewer, Jr., of Sonoma** State University kept a cheeseburger in his back pocket when he played. The burger was his good-luck charm. Dale became a big believer in burgers one night in 1995 after skipping dinner before a game. Feeling hungry at the ballpark, he asked his mom to run out to a local burger joint and get him a cheeseburger. By the time she returned, the game had started. Dale ate some of the burger in the on-deck circle, then stuffed the rest of it in his back pocket. He went to the plate, dug in, and smacked a double. After that, Dale had a burger on his buns during every game the rest of the season.

◄ **Harness racehorse Manfred Hanover won** 16 races in a row in 1985 and 1986. What was the secret of the speedy stallion's success? Sports-energy drinks. Manfred slurped about 800 quarts of them during his winning streak. He guzzled the stuff right out of the bottle. His favorite flavor: orange.

▶ **Jeff Goldman worked up a big appetite during the** 1997 Vineman Triathlon. He swam 2.4 miles and rode a bike 112 miles. Before Jeff ran the final 26.2 miles, his wife called a pizzeria and had a pepperoni pizza delivered to him in the area where the runners gathered. Jeff wolfed down two thirds of the pie, then dashed off to a personal-best time of 13 hours 9 minutes 49 seconds for the event. (He was four hours behind the winner.)

FAN-TASTIC ANTICS

What would sports be without wacky fans? A lot less interesting. Check out these events at which fans _really_ got into the action!

▼ **The St. Louis Browns let their fans manage the team during a 1951 game against the Philadelphia A's.** Coaches held up signs such as BUNT? or STEAL? Fans behind the Browns' dugout voted by holding up cards answering YES or NO. "_Fan_tastic" decisions led the Browns to a 5–3 win. The team's manager spent most of the game sipping a drink in a rocking chair!

▲ **The Boston Patriots beat the Dallas Texans,** 28–21, in an American Football League game on November 3, 1961, thanks to a clutch defensive play by . . . a Patriot fan. On the last play of the game, Dallas quarterback Cotton Davidson fired a pass toward receiver Chris Burford in the end zone. Chris was about to make the catch when the ball was batted away by a fan who had sneaked onto the field. The fan ran away before the refs saw him, so the play was ruled an incomplete pass.

FAN-TASTIC ANTICS

▶ **"Gonna Fly Now" is the theme song from** the famous boxing movie *Rocky*. Maybe it inspired the kooky fan who "crashed" the heavyweight championship bout between Evander Holyfield and Riddick Bowe on November 6, 1993. The fan strapped himself to a paraglider and swooped into the outdoor arena in Las Vegas, Nevada, during Round 7. He crashed into the side of the ring and got tangled in the ropes. The fight was delayed for 21 minutes while the fan was untangled, then arrested by police.

▶ **Nice try, guys. The Chicago Blackhawks** and the New York Americans were tied at one goal apiece in the 1938 Stanley Cup semi-finals in New York's Madison Square Garden. Winger Alex Levinsky fired a puck into New York's net to put the Blackhawks up, 2–1. But the goal light didn't go on. A group of New York fans had grabbed the goal judge's hands and prevented him from turning on the light. Alex's goal counted, of course, and the Blackhawks went on to win the game.

▶ **New York Yankee shortstop Derek Jeter hit a deep fly ball** in Game 1 of the 1996 American League Division Series at Yankee Stadium. As Baltimore Oriole rightfielder Tony Tarasco went to make the catch, a 12-year-old boy stuck his glove over the wall. The ball bounced off the glove and into the stands. The Orioles argued that Derek was out because of fan interference. But the umps hadn't seen the ball hit the kid's glove, so they ruled the hit a homer.

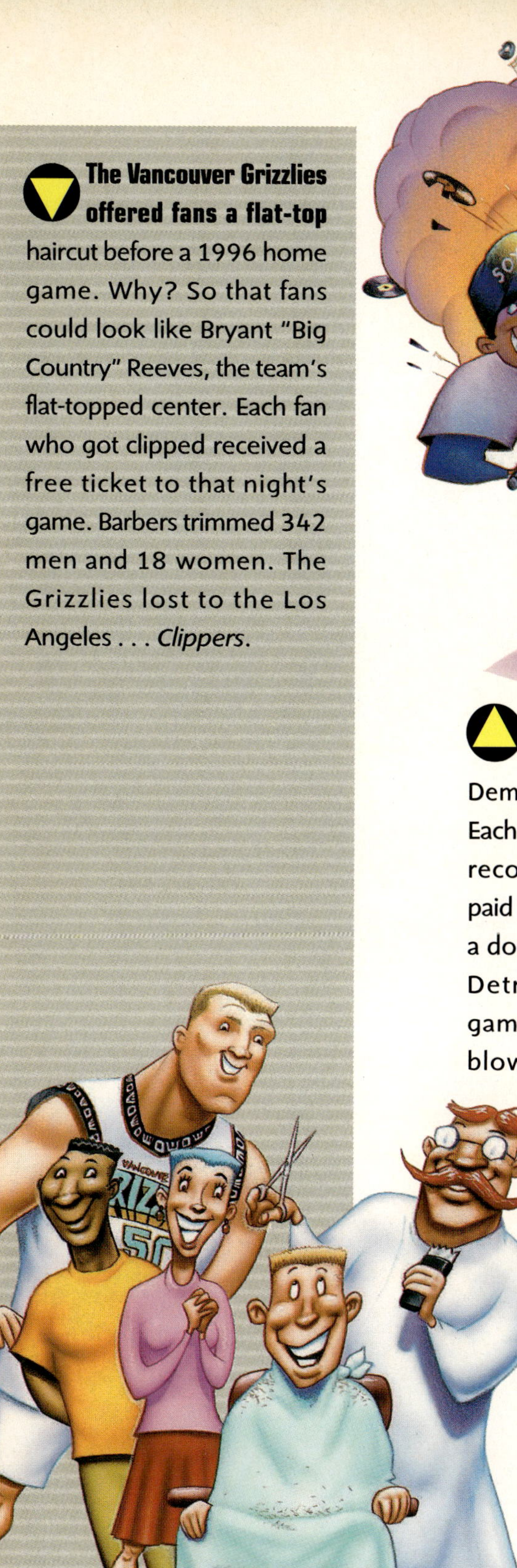

The Vancouver Grizzlies offered fans a flat-top haircut before a 1996 home game. Why? So that fans could look like Bryant "Big Country" Reeves, the team's flat-topped center. Each fan who got clipped received a free ticket to that night's game. Barbers trimmed 342 men and 18 women. The Grizzlies lost to the Los Angeles . . . *Clippers*.

The Chicago White Sox had a blast on Disco Demolition Night, in 1979. Each fan who brought disco records to Comiskey Park paid only 98 cents to watch a doubleheader against the Detroit Tigers. Between games, the records were blown up with dynamite. Chicago had to forfeit the second game after rowdy fans ran onto the field after the explosion.

Talk about a cranky call! During the first round of the 1991 Doral-Ryder Open golf tournament, in Miami, Florida, a TV viewer in Colorado spotted golfer Paul Azinger breaking a rule. Paul was kicking stones away from his ball before taking a shot on the final hole. The viewer called tournament officials and told them that Paul should be penalized two strokes for illegally moving an impediment. The officials reviewed a videotape of the telecast and saw the caller was right. Paul was disqualified because he had signed his scorecard without deducting two strokes, the penalty required by the PGA for the rule he broke.

ANIMALS AND MASCOTS

Sports mascots are supposed to be fun, colorful, and exciting. But some have been just plain strange.

▶ **The Saskatchewan Roughriders of the Canadian Football League had a very hot mascot in the 1980's: The Flame. The Flame really fired up** crowds at Roughrider home games. Each time the team scored, a 12-to-15-foot flame shot up from the top of his helmet! But one day a young fan got too close to The Flame and was burned. Team officials put out The Flame for good.

▲ **What is it? That's what people asked when** the mascot for the 1996 Summer Olympics was introduced. The mascot was a big, fat, blue blob. It's name was . . . Whatizit!

Fans were not excited by Whatizit because they couldn't figure out what Whatizit was supposed to be!

The mascot's designers had to go back to their drawing board before the Olympics opened. Whatizit was given a sleeker body and a sleeker name: Izzy. But fans still wondered: "What *was* he . . . or she?"

The Kansas City A's mascot in the 1960's was a mule named Charlie O. He was named after the team's owner, Charles O. Finley. The mule went on the field at home games. He even traveled with the team on road trips. Mr. Finley once rode Charlie O. through the lobby of a New York City hotel!

In 1968, the A's moved to Oakland, California. Charlie O. trotted off to retirement eight years later, in 1976.

The Washington Bullets (now the Wizards) were a bad team between 1989 and 1996. Their mascot was bad, too. "Hoops" looked like a garbage can and acted trashy. He was thrown out of a game for urging the crowd to heckle the ref. He got in trouble for whacking a kid with a plastic baseball bat. In 1997, the Bullets wisely sank Hoops.

The crazy Crab of Candlestick Park became the San Francisco Giants' mascot in 1985. He tried hard, but The Crab couldn't butter up the fans. They simply hated mascots. For fun, the Giants encouraged the fans to boo and yell insults, such as "Boil it!" The poor shell-shocked Crab lasted only one season.

WEIRD WEATHER

Rain, snow, and high wind can be unbeatable opponents. Here's what can happen when weird weather comes to call.

The Boston Bruins and Edmonton Oilers played a steamy Game 4 of the Stanley Cup finals on May 24, 1988. Boston Garden had no air-conditioning. The arena temperature rose to 108 degrees, and the ice began to melt. The water vapor turned into fog. The players could barely see the puck. But they played on — until a power failure put out the lights!

A blizzard buried Washington, D.C., before a 1960 game between the Washington Redskins and the New York Giants. A foot of snow made the tarp covering the field too heavy to pull off. So the teams played on top of the snowy tarp. The Giants rushed for only one yard, but they came out on tarp, er, on *top*, 17–3!

"

▼ **Unusually warm weather thawed out the 1988** Winter Olympics. First, most of the snow around Calgary, Alberta, Canada, melted. Next, fierce 98-mile-per-hour winds blew sand and dirt from nearby hills onto the ice-covered bobsled course. The two-man bobsled event had to be postponed until the following evening, when Mother Nature put Calgary back into its usual deep freeze.

▲ **Basketball games are rarely washed out.** So the Washington Bullets and Phoenix Suns were surprised to see water seeping through the floor of US Air Arena before the Bullets' 1994 home game. The arena was so warm that the hockey-rink ice under the court was melting. The teams splashed through their warm-ups before the game was canceled.

▼ **The Houston Astros and Pittsburgh Pirates were** ready to play in the Houston Astrodome on June 15, 1976. But their *indoor* game was *rained out!* The teams got to the 'Dome before a big storm dumped 10 inches of rain and flooded roads. But fans, umps, and stadium workers couldn't get to the 'Dome!

BAD LUCK

Luck is a big part of sports. But when it turns bad, it's no fun for anyone.

▼ **Defenseman Brian Leetch of the New York Rangers should have worn his ice skates home from a 1993 game at Madison Square** Garden. Brian stepped out of a taxicab in front of his apartment in New York City. He slipped on the icy sidewalk and fell. Brian broke his right ankle and missed the final 13 games of the season.

▼ **The Tampa Bay Buccaneers joined the NFL in 1976. The** Bucs were a collection of castoffs and rejects from other NFL teams. They finished 0–14 in their first season, and they fumbled away 12 more games in 1977 before they finally won. After one terrible loss, Tampa Bay coach John McKay was asked what he thought of his team's "execution."

"I'm in favor of it," the coach joked.

▼ **The Washington Generals didn't win a basketball** game for 24 years! The Generals played the Harlem Globetrotters hundreds of times each year. During games, the Globetrotters got laughs from the crowd by playing tricks on the pitiful Generals. The Generals actually won a game on January 5, 1971. Then they lost more than 8,000 games in a row. The team broke up in 1995.

▼ **Speedy outfielder Vince Coleman of the St. Louis** Cardinals was run down by a tarpaulin that was moving at less than one mile per hour. Vince was standing near the first-base line before Game 4 of the 1985 National League Championship Series. When it began to rain, the tarp rolled out to cover the infield. The tarp hit Vince from behind and injured his left knee. He missed the rest of the series.

▲ **A safety pin poked a hole in Spectacular** Bid's bid to win horse racing's Triple Crown in 1979. He won the Crown's first two races, the Kentucky Derby and the Preakness. But he stepped on a safety pin the morning before the third race, the Belmont Stakes. The pin jammed into his left front hoof. He competed with a sore hoof and finished third.

▼ **NFL players are often injured during games.** But quarterback Neil O'Donnell of the New York Jets was knocked out of action while warming up *before a game* in 1996. Neil was practicing passing plays with the Jets' offensive team. He dropped back to pass. Suddenly, his right calf hurt so much that he could barely walk. Neil had pulled a muscle. He missed the game and the rest of the season!

▼ **During his NBA career, center Luc Longley of** the Chicago Bulls banged bodies on the court. But during the 1996-97 season, Luc was banged up himself while bodysurfing. He hit the waves during a road trip in California. A wave he was riding slammed him into the sand. Luc's left shoulder was separated. He was knocked out of action for six weeks.

"I'm lucky I didn't break my neck," said Luc.

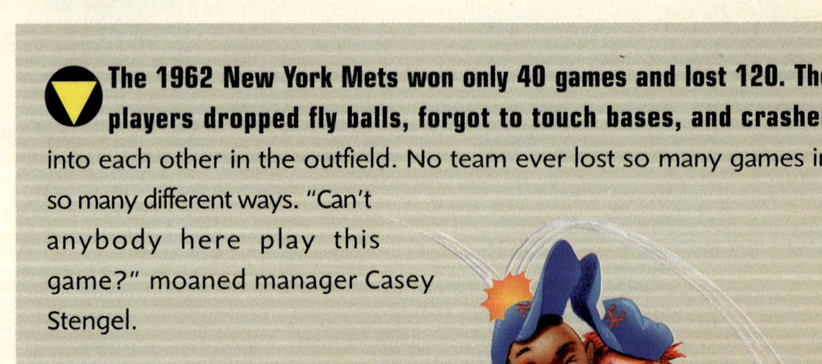

▼ **The 1962 New York Mets won only 40 games and lost 120. The players dropped fly balls, forgot to touch bases, and crashed** into each other in the outfield. No team ever lost so many games in so many different ways. "Can't anybody here play this game?" moaned manager Casey Stengel.

MAJOR MISHAPS

Athletes are ready to perform, no matter what. But sometimes things don't go as planned.

▼ For Felix Carvajal of Cuba, running the marathon at the 1904 Olympics was much easier than getting to the Games. The Olympics were held in St. Louis, Missouri. Felix took a steamship from Havana, Cuba, to New Orleans, Louisiana. But he lost all his money in New Orleans. So Felix had to hitch rides to St. Louis — 688 miles away. Luckily, Felix made it to St. Louis in time for the race. He finished fourth.

▲ Before a February 1990 game between the Chicago Bulls and the Orlando Magic, Michael Jordan's jersey vanished. The Bulls didn't have an extra number 23 jersey, so Michael wore number 12. That jersey did not have a name on the back. But fans at the game in Orlando, Florida, quickly figured out the identity of the mystery man wearing number 12. His Airness scored 49 points that night.

▼ **Fans at a 1978 NBA game were puzzled by** the oddly dressed player on the visiting team. The Washington Bullets and San Antonio Spurs were playing in Washington. Guard Mike Gale of the Spurs was wearing a Bullet road-game uniform, and he had the jersey on inside out! Mike's luggage had been lost on the trip to Washington. The Bullets let him use one of their uniforms.

▼ **A New York Met farm team pulled off a real** "squeeze play" in 1971. The Tidewater Tides were on their way to a game in Tampa, Florida. Their bus broke down with five miles to go. The Tides called a taxi service, but only four cabs were available. No problem. Forty players, coaches, and team officials — and all the team's equipment — squeezed into the four cabs, and off they went!

▲ **At a 1975 track meet, U.S. sprinter Steve** Riddick won a 60-yard dash wearing heavy sweatpants. Later, reporters asked Steve why he hadn't taken off his sweatpants at the starting line and run in his shorts. The answer? Steve had left his shorts in his hotel room!

NICKNAMES

**Some pro sports teams got their nicknames
in unusual ways**

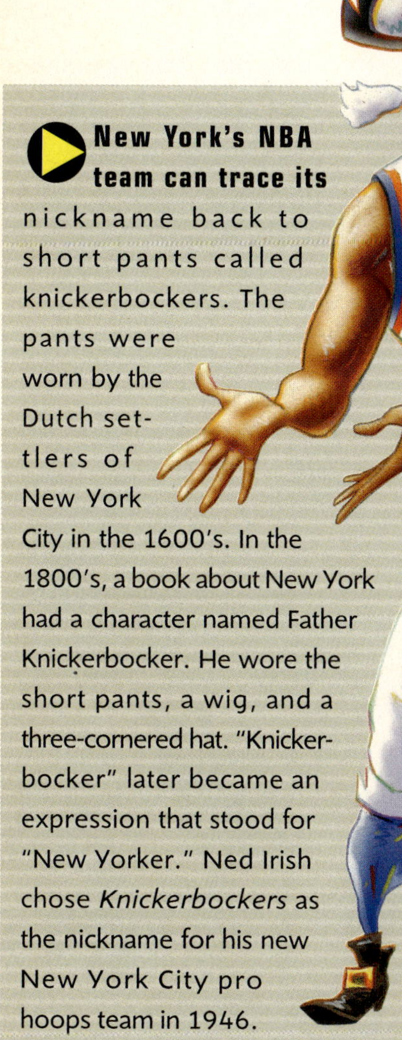

New York's NBA team can trace its nickname back to short pants called knickerbockers. The pants were worn by the Dutch settlers of New York City in the 1600's. In the 1800's, a book about New York had a character named Father Knickerbocker. He wore the short pants, a wig, and a three-cornered hat. "Knicker-bocker" later became an expression that stood for "New Yorker." Ned Irish chose *Knickerbockers* as the nickname for his new New York City pro hoops team in 1946.

What are the Los Angeles Dodgers supposed to be dodging? Trolley cars! There are no trolleys in Los Angeles. But the Dodgers used to play in Brooklyn, which is a borough of New York City. In the 1890's, people in Brooklyn rode trolley cars the way they now ride buses. Pedestrians crossing the crowded streets had to dodge the trolleys. Brooklyn's team was named the Trolley Dodgers. Over time, the name was shortened to "Dodgers." The team kept its name after it moved to Los Angeles, California, in 1957.

► **Earl "Curly" Lambeau worked in a meat-packing** plant in Green Bay, Wisconsin. In 1919, he decided to form a pro football team. The owner of the Indian Packing Company gave Curly $500 to buy uniforms and equipment. Curly thanked the owner by naming the team the Packers. Curly coached Green Bay for 29 seasons.

▼ **The Pittsburgh Pirates were called the** Alleghenies until 1891. That year, they were accused of stealing a player from the Philadelphia Athletics. The Athletics had accidentally left second baseman Lou Bierbauer off a list of players who were protected from being claimed by other teams. When Pittsburgh claimed Lou, the Athletics called the Alleghenies "pirates" for stealing him. The nickname stuck.

▼ **Talk about a bolt of inspiration! In 1990, an NHL team was created in Tampa, Florida. Phil Esposito was the** team's general manager. His team needed a nickname. One day, Phil was eating lunch at a restaurant that overlooks Tampa Bay. Suddenly, a bolt of lightning flashed in the sky. "I knew right then that I had the perfect name for the team," says Phil. He named the team the Tampa Bay Lightning.